AF552331

The River

Ma Jaya Sati Bhagavati

GANGA PRESS

ROSELAND, FLORIDA

Published by: Ganga Press
11155 Roseland Rd.
Sebastian, FL 32958

Editorial and design: Mukunda

Publisher's Cataloging in Publication
(Prepared by Quality Books Inc.)

Ma, Jaya Sati Bhagavati.
The river / Jaya Sati Bhagavati Ma.
p. cm.
ISBN 0-9640469-0-3

1. Ganges River (India and Bangladesh)--Poetry.
I. Title.
PS3563.M353R5 1994 811'.54
QBI94-440

Photo Credits:
Ma in the Ganges: Hanuman Giri
Ma in Arizona: Durga Stroll

First printing, May, 1994
Printed in USA

Written in honor of my Guru,
Neem Karoli Baba

In memory of my Naga Baba,
Billy

...and for you, Chela

Ma in the Ganges at Hardwar

1977

I have taken it upon myself to bring to the many the beauty of my River, the Ganga—the sacredness of her abundance, the joy of her waters, and the fact that her holiness can and does heal the hearts of humanity's sorrow in this time of the AIDS plague.

My River and all her aspects or streams cool the aching, longing heart of the seeker. Whatever the religion of the one who screams out to the Mother to be held, my River can hear. Her very being grants grace amongst the holy and forgiveness for the sinner. Her home is Kashi, the holiest city in all of India, some say in all the world. I write this poetry from the place in my heart that stores the waters of the Ganga and allows me to flow freely in my teachings.

The mist of the Mother Earth comes from her daughter, the Ganga, the abundant River that nourishes all of mankind and the gods and goddesses. I bow to my Mother, the Ganga. May her waters quench the thirst of humanity's needs. May we all swim in her flowing waters of compassion and truth.

The worship of my River is so very old
Her story must be told
I shall worship and tell of she I bow to
Mother Gangé, I shall tell of you

The River of my dreams lives and flows in the
    City of Lights
Her blanket is Kashi
Her soul is Shiva
Her sister is Kali
I, Ma, am her daughter
I, Ma, thirst for her water
I shall drink my fill and then drink more
I shall give what I have consumed to my sons
    and daughters
Her riverfront shrines shall live in my heart
The Holy walk down Kashi's narrow ancient streets
Behind the dead they walk repeating the name of my
    Mother Gangé
Her name comes to the near-dead
I place her tilak upon the dead's head

They all come to my River
The rich and the poor swim in her waters
Some wear new gold and silver bought in Kashi's markets
Some come to drink her sacred fluid
Some come to be blessed
Some come to die
Some come to laugh
Some come to wash their garments
Others come only to bathe and be blessed
All know that the moment is sacred—
Sacred moment, sacred waters
Sacred River, sacred streams

The dead float down the River
Ash spread thick on the breast of my River
Manikarnika Ghat burns all the day by my River
Manikarnika Ghat burns all the night by my River
Kali watches the fires and yearns for her children to die
before death
I love my River's cooling heat upon my body
I bow to my Mother, the Ganga
I bow to her waters in the now

A morning bath in my River soothes the day
    that is yet to begin
The naked flesh begins free of sin
The River waters—always to dry in the sun
A clean, simple cloth spread upon the body
    and the puja's done

The shadow of the linga spreads upon Shiva's spouse
The shadow dances with the River and with the reflection
    of the sacred cow
The white bull dances, too
The white bull dances, too
Bow low, sadhu, to the bull in you

There, by the water's edge, is a temple
    to the Monkey God
The Holy are putting garlands around his head
I bow to the Son of the Wind, Hanuman
There, in his face, is my Guru's grace
There, in his face, is my Guru's face
I bow to my Baba, the son of the Ganga
Her husband and father too
I bow to Lord Ganesha, the god who removes obstacles

The children play by my River
As the Holy pray by my River
The seeker spends his day by my River
The Holy spend their lives by my River
The children grow up in the wet of the River
It is the children who learn to want the Giver
The little ones swim with the dead
in the River of their youth
It is the children who know from their Mother,
the Ganga, truth
Learn to whisper in the dying's ear the name of God—the
Mother shares this thought with her
little hearts
They listen to the Sacred Mother and flow in their youth
to the source of life
It is the children by the River's bank who get life right
Children playing by the River's waters

As the River's sons and daughters flow in the form of ash
past their own youthful homes
The living and the dead—at the Mother's breast
Neither are ever alone

Children, play by my River
Sadhu, stay by my River
A good death promised all by my River
The dead are wrapped in red or white
The ash will be spread on the River this very night
Kali will come and dance in the burning ghats
She will sear and soak the sacred flames of lifetimes past
Her singed tiger skin will wear pieces of her singed hair

I, Ma, at times wish I were there
Yet I have brought to the West the very essence of Kali's River
I have brought the burning ghats and the floating corpse
I have brought the pujaris and the sacred flame of the lost

Children, come play in my River
Sadhu, come stay by my River
Cities so very old by my River
Temples shine with their gold by my River
Cows stray all the day by my River
So many come to die by my River

My lota is filled with my River's waters taken
by the River

I carry the ash in the lota's waters

I splash the ash upon the dead's survivors

The River flows to the point of Shiva's Bay of Bengal

No one of the River knows hell

Kashi casts her mystical spell on all that is in need
of the Mother's waters

Eyes closed, I see inside of me the fullness of the River
that I was meant to be

It is in these modern times that I cry out into the night,

I am She! I am She!

Shiva lifts his mighty hands and blesses all
of Kashi's lands

Shiva lifts his trident and the arrogant become bent

The River that flowed from Shiva's jetta locks
wears the dead as her frock

My Mother, the Ganga, always flowing
with her abundant breasts of milky white

As the children come and play by her waters I,
the Naga Baba, come and pray by her waters

All the Holy come and stay by her waters as the sacredness
of the cows strays by her waters

I am the Ganga's son by her waters

It is the sacred rudraksha bead that saves the lineage
of the Ganga

Come, child, and be the one who is wild in her waters

The water buffalo lie down in the waters

The children jump off their backs and splash
the holy wetness making the Mother
laugh in delight

The scent of jasmine and musk permeates
the River night

The less holy take flight

The pyres burn bright

The scent of burning flesh is what the River sadhu
loves best

Another death in Kashi, another death
at the water's edge

Another life about to be born

Old Man, don't cry

Did I not die by my River?

Was I not born by my River?

I am the River child

I thirst for the waters

I thirst for the waters even as I am neck deep
in her sacred wetness

I am witness to Kali's prancing on the body of Shiva

He is the stillness of the River's heart

Kashi, my blood runs thick with your River's waters

Two thoughts come together, Shiva Shakti become one

Kashi and the Ganga are where the original thought
comes from

So, come my little ones and play all the day by my River

The ash-covered Naga will keep you safe as you run wild
at the River's edge

So safe the ash feels upon my breast

So safe the wet

The River has given so many their final rest
The River can bring a peaceful newness
The old come to become young again
The young come to receive the wisdom of age
My River has been home to the sinner and the sage

Children, come play in my River
Sadhu, come stay by my River
The gentle come to pray by my River
My life has led me to the River's bank
I stay here and serve all who can hear
Hear of the River and her gods and goddesses
So much to teach, so much to share.
When the children hurt from this world
I take them to my River and show them love unspoiled

Can you hear me, Mother? I am whispering in the night
As I sit by the bedside of one who is finished this life
All I can say is the River Song

Words that can soothe, waters that can heal
The River flows through my breast
I have become my Mother and her song

I watch as the beggar and the king swim in my Mother's
waters side by side
The Guru teaching Tantra in the moonlit night
The father sending the corpse of his dead baby afloat
on the water's surface
The bloated dead water buffalo floating
in the River's stream
Charas coming from the old sadhu's pipe,
giving him a River dream

I cry out as I sit on the River's bank,
Mother Kali with the disheveled hair
Know my children are here!
Her black form merges with my soul
I am happy in my River life, happy just to be

Kali's name is nectar to my heart
Here in Kashi on the banks on the River Ganga
Kali is the goddess worshipped by the River child
Kali, the terrifying; Kali, the wild

Children, come play in the waters of the sacred Ganga
Take hold of the Black One's hand
Be free of the bondage of life in your youth
Be free even in your desire for truth
Sadhu, as you stay on my River's edge, think of the
Dark One and how she bled
Children, as you gather your years
Gather not the world's poison or fears
Sink into the well of Kali's destiny
Sink into the River's whirlpool of life
All must be children at the breast of Ganga
Kali shall destroy all dangers as you sit with legs crossed
on the banks of the River
Jai Gangé! Victory to the River and her children!
By the River we are all her sons and daughters

His being has touched my own
We two sit by the Ganga always at home
Those who come to our water's edge
Find moksha from within

Even the water buffalo taste liberation
The Mother honors all things that honor the waters

I sit with my Baba and know I am the water's daughter
The sky over Kashi is filled with birds of the highest order
The lowly rodent has a place at Shiva's side in this
  wondrous place of Kashi
My River never runs dry in this place of Kashi
They come to worship life in this place of Kashi
They come to worship death in this place of Kashi

The dhuni burns bright
  as I place the sacred bark of the neem tree
  into the flames to represent me
My ash shall blow in the wind over the River Gangé
Vayu shall carry the ash to all who worship the Mother
The naked Naga shall tell of this time in another time and
  clime until his ashes merge with mine

Go, said the formless god of Brahma, who was none other
than himself,
Go and make Kashi a world unto itself

And who shall rule this world?

The god answered,
The Formless, who housed the Ganga in his curls

Shiva came to claim his home
On the banks of the Ganga
Shiva merged with her waters
Remembering when she could not shake herself free
Shiva bowed to the Mother and restored her dignity
His consort Uma came to be on the banks of the Ganga
Shiva, the destroyer of all things
Learned to build once again for those who survived
the death of the ego

All others cried and died and were sent to dry shores

Until Uma cried out and said,

No worse hell could be found than to be away
from the River's shores

Come sinners and swim in my Mother's waters as children at
the breast

In Kashi by the Ganga there are no tests

All are welcome to be nurtured by her daughter Annapurna

No one shall starve in the land of Kashi

I am Uma, said the Earth Mother

And this I decree

Death came upon Kashi and saw he had power no more

Children, come play by my River and see Yama bow
to his Lord

Yama bows to Shiva of the Ganga, and Death swims
with the children of the Ganga

All live with the Mother Ganga

Every once in a while my heart longs to return to the sacred
land of Kashi

To taste her waters and swim inside of me

Then my eyes close and it is so simple to see

The River's essence always flows free

I hear the River call her children to witness
Mother Kali's dance of the skulls

She begins her dance at the River's edge

Children who are playing in the River stop and dry off
in the hot Kashi sun

Sadhus sit straight before Mother Kali, the one they adore

Cities seem ancient as Kali's dance begins

Temples glow in the shadow of their own gold

Cows stop straying before Kali's dance

Sannyasi stop praying; Kali is the prayer

Sinners and saints come from everywhere

The sun goes down upon the Gangé

Kali takes her devotee away

Away to the cremation ground to finish her River dance

On the corpse does the Black Mother dance

Shiva hears her dimmie dimmies and joins her beneath
    the night sky

I am here, the Ashen One cries out,

To dance the dance of the skulls

Who will lead in this dance of the Manikarnika Ghat?
It is Kali speaking to her spouse

You shall, Dark One, and I, Shiva, shall lay still—

I, your consort, shall follow your will

The Ashen One lay down upon the dead
Kali placed her feet upon his chest
The dead danced with the dead
The living danced with ash upon their heads
The night brought the stars overhead
Chela brought Guru garlands of night-blooming jasmine
All ran to the waters to be blessed
Kali danced in the waters up to her chest
Shiva lay still in the midst of the dead
Mother Ganga laughed and played with her children
Her waters flowed free
Her waters were warmed in Kashi's night breeze

Oh, Kali, the River sang out
Keep Shiva still under your feet

The devotee cried into the night, *Oh, Kali, come and dance*
with me!

Remember, sang the Ganga,
When you were all children in my River
Remember, she sang, *when I taught you of the Giver*
Remember when you, the child, became the sadhu who sat
by my River
Running wild to and fro by my River
Remember the flames that danced from my dhuni
Remember, my chela, to always know me

The first light of the day made himself known
Dancers wearing the bone all went home to the caves of Kashi
The Ashen One went with me
Come, my children, set the night free
Kali, Kali, will you now sleep?

Nay, said the Dark One,

Now it is time to just be

I will sit by the River

I will wait and see who will come to my
Mother Ganga in the first light of dawn

I will watch who will ask of Shiva for me

I will be the children swimming in the River

I will be the sadhu sitting by the River

I will be the city old by the River

I will be the temple gold by the River

I will be the cow that strays by the River

I will be the story told by the River

I will never grow old by the River

I will watch Shiva grow bold by the River

I will be all who die by the River

I will be the widow who cries by the River

I will be Ma Bhagavati by the River, always sitting
with the Giver

Always blessed by the River

Always Kali of the River

I bow to my Mother, the waters of the River

He who drinks the nectar from the feet of the Mother
    surely knows the River
Her magic lies in the beauty of the River
River, hear my song
River, hear my cry
River, hear my heart
River, hear my pain
River, hear my joy
River, hear my children in the waters of your River
They splash and play with their Mother, the Ganga
To be a child again is the ultimate lila of Shiva
To be in the Mother's lap at all times is to be the child
    of the River

How, Mother, do they know you?
Can I sing your praises to those who will hear?
Can I tell of your compassion and your removal of fear?
    Fear from your children's hearts
    Fear from life's horrors

My Mother, I shall tell of you all my life
How you welcome the children of the night
Giving unconditional love to all those who call your name
Mother, I shall tell of your fame
To be in the warmth of your waters repeating your holy name
OM Namah Gangé!
OM Namah Shivaya!

My Mother
My Father
River of my heart
The sages teach of your ways
As the children constantly play in the River
The sadhus sitting so close to the River's edge fear neither
life nor death
Bhairava, Shiva's own essence, eats karma as the pilgrims
drink of the River
Temples of Kala Bhairava line the banks of Mother's waters
I kneel in the sacred mud, proud to be Ganga's daughter

I watch the old wrinkled one pranam to Mother
    on the water's edge
She walks with sinking breast into the flow
Her face fills out, her breasts rise high
Her jetta hair flows brilliant black
She is Kali ridding herself of the cremation ground's karma
The night has left her old in the sun
The waters fill her flesh with the youth she has given up
Milk fills her breast

By cow dust time Mahakali is ready to ride Shiva in the
    graveyard of dead thoughts
The Ganga has filled her being once more
The mystery of Kashi is born from Kali's mind
She is beauty and passion
She is love and in her darkness Kashi is the light
The River has made her ready for the night
The candles, lit and placed on the leaves to float down
    till dawn
Kali once again is born

My Mother, my sister, my lover, my friend
You, the Black One, eat all beginnings and devour all ends
I sit on the steps to the ghat before the piers
My back can feel the heat of the fires
My feet are cooled in Ganga's waters

There before me a sadhu's corpse floats past
He seems to laugh
He has sat by the River watching the children play beneath the ancient city
He has sat in the shadow of temples made of gold
He became old by the River and could be no more, his jetta hair down to the floor
He took his last breath as Vishwanatha whispered RAM in his ear
Then all life disappeared
He was a holy sadhu
The Shiva knot on the top of his head showed he was Shaivite, too

Kashi is his home for all his lives.

At death the ash on his form began to fall into
his Mother's waters
Vishwanatha gently pushed him in the River
For the sadhu cannot be burned by my River
He must be consumed by the Mother
Her waters must become his sight
Her waters must become his soul
In her waters the sadhu becomes whole
Her wisdom becomes his bed for next life

The Holy One awakens with Kali at his side
Mother, Mother, how long have you been with me?
How long have you witnessed my misery?
I have called out to you since the beginning of time
My Mother, did I need the River to tell you of me?

The sadhu lies at the wet feet of Mother Kali
Her feet have soaked up the River
Nectar drips from her toes as she walks the River's banks
At this moment the sadhu has awoken to give thanks

Thank you, my Ganga, for your waters have made me whole
Thank you, my Mother, for your waters have made Kali bold
Thank you, my River, for your story now to be told

Come now, my heart, let you and I sit in solitude
I am sure my Mother Kali will follow me as long as I follow the River's stream
I thank the Ganga for my life as a sadhu
As a child I played in the River, watching the Holy as they sat by the River
The water buffalo leaped in my River
The elephants drank from my River
The cows strayed by my River all the day by my River
I have become a devotee of the waters of my River
I shall drink the honey in the city of Kashi
I shall whisper my Mother's name till kingdom come
I am my Mother's son
You have given me your breast, my Mother, at the River's edge
I have drunk my fill in Kashi
How long have you been beside me, my Mother Kali?

I have been there all your lifetimes though you have not
noticed me
I have been the wind in the trees
I have been the wood in the dhuni
I have been the water in the lota
I have been the stars in the sky
The sun up high
The moon in the night
Yet all you did is call out my name
Never did you listen as Shiva did the same
If you had heard Mahadeva's voice
You would see I had no choice but to come to all who call
me at the River's edge
I can do no less

I watched the children playing by my River
I watched you, the sadhu, staying by my River
Then I watched you become the child playing again
by the River
I slept at your side where I have always been in Kashi
Only by becoming a child did you have the power
to notice me

Tell me, my Mother, is it true that I was so occupied being a
good sadhu that I forgot to be a simple child calling you?

Yes, my son, that is the lila of Shiva's dance

You call out for the dance so long that one forgets to hear
the secret sound of the damaru

Come, my son, and I shall show you

The Black Mother walked down the River's steps taking
hold of the sadhu's hand

All who prayed by the River's edge could only see
a lonely sadhu talking to the Ganga,
his hand outstretched like a child

The sadhu had a look of ecstasy as he entered
into the River of Bliss

The Dark Mother and her son became one by my River

Mother, Mother, never leave me, said the Oneness
in the River

How can I leave myself? the Black One sang

And the River Song was born

In the beginning there was only the River that lived high
in the heavens
Humanity needed her waters to live
Humanity needed her waters to die
She was sent by the gods with all her arrogance to leap
to the earth
Her power was too strong for the land
So Lord Shiva was asked to stand
She came rambling toward sacred land
Into his hair did she flow
Shiva laughed and laughed
She tried to shake loose—Shiva paid her no heed
Then the River relaxed and the Lord Shankara tried to
shake her loose
The two together became consorts
The two together became the world

The River flows gently in her own time
Each River child says out loud in Kashi,
The River is all mine

Silence comes to those who sit on the banks of the River
That silence is the power of Shakti
Guru and chela sit as one beneath the neem tree
Thoughts melt
Sounds disappear
Night into day
God is near
Annapurna appears
Guru and chela become one
The River Song is done

The River flows on and on taking the Oneness with her
All is the same, all is different
All have tasted the waters, the waters that never change

The storekeeper hawks his wares
The young women wash their hair
The Holy sit so still by the River's edge
They are bound for moksha in their city of Kashi
Has anyone noticed that Guru and chela have become one?
Just as the song that has just been sung
And the song shall go on, even when the singing is done

A child plays on the stairs going from the village to the River
In his heart the beat goes to the tune of:
I have always been here

A dead baby, too young to be burned on the funeral pyre
Floats down its Mother Ganga
All this is Shakti, all this is the Mother
The River is the mirror of the sky
Men doing puja in the early morn
This is the River's song

Murtis being washed in the sacred waters

Kali walking silently on the River's edge, looking for her
 sons and daughters

There, by the burning ghat, bodies burn day and night

There, in the burning ghat, souls lift to God as Shiva,
 the Destroyer, stands guard

The eyes of the corpses open wide before the River's fires
 consume them

Kali shall dance on my ashes, they sing into the pyres

They are glad to be dead by the River's edge

Their lives are through—no more breath

Only the joy of their Mother playing with their skulls
 as if they were toys

Mother, may I dance this night with you
 in the cremation ground of my youth?

Shiva laughs and says,

Have you consumed Kali this life?

Have you called out her name in the moments of joy
 or have you only looked for your Mother
 in moments of grief?

Now you want the Black One to dance upon your bones
When in life you never called the cremation ground your home

The River, hearing this exchange of words
Calls out to Shiva,
How absurd!
I am their Mother—they have no other
and if they cannot consume my daughter in life
they shall try beneath the crescent moon of their Father!

Saying these words, the Ganga calls on Ganesha to remove the obstacles of life for the dead
The River child plays by the River all the days of the River
The sadhus stay by the River
Ganesha sings the River Song loud and clear
His father, Shiva, begins his dance with the damaru in his hand
The waters explode with anticipation of Shiva's movements

Uma arrives from the Earth that caught her at death
Lie still, Lord Shiva, so Kali can dance on your chest

The fires surrounding the Lord's dance were extinguished
by the god Vayu's breath
Shiva lay down in the shade of the neem tree
Kali appeared as the sun disappeared
Upon the chest of her beloved did she step
The Ganga cried out, *Not yet!*

All was silent in the city of Kashi
All eyes were turned to the mountains high
An old woman and a much older man were walking
down the mountain hand-in-hand
He was taking her to Kashi to die
He didn't even ask why
For he knew, yes he knew

The birds sang out the River's Song
As the day died completely, Kali began to dance
  upon the still chest of her consort
Tantra was born from the River Song
The old one sat by the River for a year and a day
Not for a moment did her Lord stray
They watched, day after day
The children playing by the River

They themselves laughed and sang by the River
Gangé, you could hear the two old ones say
The River blessed them in the holiness of her waters
The River blessed her son and daughter
Her husband and sister
Her Mother, Her Lord
The earth bowed to the River it adored
The night became holy and free
The River and her song became me

The River is strong as she runs over the rocks
placed by Shiva to tame her

Nothing can stop the River as she disregards all obstacles

The storms of man's mind can be flooded
by the Ganga's own flow

The waters know, the waters know

The sadhu whispers to his mind,

Please, oh mind, never forget the Mother River

Please, oh mind, never forget her spouse, the Lord Shiva

The mind is then drenched

The soul is then soaked

Life becomes death to the ego

It cannot swim in the Ganga

Her waters are too swift

The waters are her gift

Come children, come and play in my waters
Come sadhu, come sit by my waters
Watch the cities grow old by my waters
Watch the temples gold shine by my waters
Watch the sacred cows stray by my waters
Watch the fires in the ghat not let the bodies decay
by my waters
Watch the widows cry by my waters

Tears fill my River
The tears awaken the Giver
I hear the sannyasi say,
Mother, Mother, I am burning
Mother, Mother, I am yearning

Tara comes into the waters and gives her breast freely
At that moment the River runs white with the milk
of the Mother
On the other side the Mother sings out,
There is only the sun and never clouds

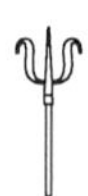

Can I enter in your boat, Mother? asks her River child

Will you carry me across, my Mother, so my spirit cannot be lost?

The River's daughter asks the Holy One,

When you drown your ego and get to the other side

When the time is ready, will you leave that place to walk at Tara's side?

When the holiness of it all fills you to your heart's content, will you be able to answer 'I will?'

I will return to where the bodies burn

I will return to where good karma has to be earned

I will go where the Mother needs to be black

I will return to where man forgets the Mother's breast

I will, my Mother, if only you will let me come into Tara's boat and go across to where the soul cannot get lost

You are the essence of all my thoughts, my Mother Tara

Do not turn your child adrift in a place without your face

Mother, anchor your boat to my heart so that when I say to the gods,

'I will leave this place'

Let the gods know that the Ganga swims in my heart

Mother, do not let the boat filled with my own karma sink into the dry place of hell

Let my mind always remember the children playing in the River

Let it never forget the sadhu in ash by my River

I have drunk the wine of life—it has turned bitter in my bowels

I have drunk the white substance from my Mother's breast

So full have I become at the water's edge

Each dawn I cry into the River,

Mother, I am your son

Let me know your waters

Let me be you, Mother

On your own banks I shall become you, my Mother

And when the time comes I shall say to all the gods

I shall leave this place and walk among the living once again

Yet the road I travel shall always be drenched in my Mother's waters

I shall leave this place

Yet as I step on the soil of Kashi I will know, I will know

I will know the scent of my River

I will know the sound of the children who laugh in my River

I will sing praises of my Mother all the day

And, when cow dust time approaches, I shall call the night mine

I shall follow the water's edge to the cremation ground

I shall follow the dripping blood coming from my Mother Kali's mouth

I shall enter into the fires of the Manikarnika Ghat

I shall become the dead

My bones shall rid themselves of life's flesh

I shall be carried upon my Mother's chest

I shall be the poet of Mother Ganga and write in her own blood her song of love

And when the hyena begins his love song for the flesh he wants to devour

I shall laugh in his face and tell the beast to hurry, for my bones long for my Mother's neck

All this shall occur in Kashi

All this shall happen by my River

As the children ride the water buffalo into the flowing waters of Gangé

Were they ever young, these River children?

Did they know when they jumped and laughed that sometimes the laughter does not last unless the mind can be splashed by the waters of the sacred River?

I will wish to be Shava, the corpse of Shiva, in the cremation ground

I shall listen to the River and all her sounds

I shall lay in the stillness of death

I shall lay like a corpse as my Mother, my spouse, dances wildly upon my chest

All this will happen by my River

My River, my life
The River of death, the River of strife
The River of the old
The River of the bold
The River whose story must be told
I shall become her poet
I, the daughter of Kali, the daughter of the Ganga
I shall dress myself in her waters
I shall use as my ink her child Kali's blood
Her blood will tell her story of love
And when I, the poet of the River, hear these words,
    Who will leave this place?
I shall answer in truth, *What place?*
No place, my heart will reply
For there is no difference between life and death when
    the poet sits on the water's edge

Jai Ma! Jai Kali! Jai Gangé!
I will never leave my River
In Kashi on the banks of the Gangé is where I will always
    stay for a year and a day
For a year and a day

We who sit in Kashi sit in awe of the gods
This city of Shiva is indeed the holy of holies
How wonderful to be the receiver of the Mother's power
here upon the earth
The River flows, touching all, becoming all
Shiva smiles on those who worship the River that once took
residence in his jetta hair
All who looked for the crescent moon saw the watery
goddess dwelling there
All those who dip three times in the Ganga can easily
invoke Shiva's blessings
He insures good lives to all the children who play
in the River
He is there protecting the sadhu who is staying by the River
He is the prayer of the sannyasi who is praying by the River
He is the god of the laundry walla who feeds his children
by working in the River
He blesses the new bride who comes to the River
to be purified
He stands beside the groom as he takes his vows
by the River

Subtle is the way of the River Kali

Wild is the way of the cremation ground, Black Mother

The mystery of creation manifests itself out of the void of death

To the striving Sadhu she says, *Not yet, not yet*

To the child she explains, *Wait a while*

To the simple adult devotee she holds out her arms and exclaims, *Now, my child, come*

The two dance into the Gangé

Child, says the Black One, *do you know me?*

The simple one replies under the sun,
You are my Mother, my Mataji
You are the one who can set the dead free
You are all that I want and all that I ever want to be

Will you drown for me? asks the Black One

I would die for you, Mother.
I would live for you, Mother
I love only you; I know no other

What if you call upon yourself Shiva's wrath?

The simple one says,
That would be grace to see Shiva's face
It does not matter if he is the wrathful one
If I am the Mother's child, then I am Shiva's son

Mother and child look toward the setting sun
Come with me, she tells the holy one

They run like children along the banks of the River
They come upon the temple that houses the linga on the west bank
Kali bows low
The simple one gives thanks
Shiva, Shiva, Mahadeva! sings out the Bloody One
From the linga comes Bhairava, the Wrathful One,
Whoever dares call me while I am in the linga shall be the one to silence the dance
He sees it is his consort, Kali

Upon seeing her he calls his bull who is grazing by the River
Nandi drinks his fill of the waters
Kali and Shiva jump upon the great white one's back
The simple one sheds one tear
So great is the bliss to have his Mother and Father so near
The River sighs and rises to wash clean the dead
The ashes flow into the waters
Ganga gently fills the breast of her daughter
She calls out to her own Mother Himalaya,

Mother of the mountains, Mother of the sky

I will drench the dead and the dead will never be born dry

Night has fallen upon the River
The dead lay still, decaying flesh eaten by the roaring fires of future karma's store of wood

It is the simple one who stands in awe and speaks out to the night,

I understand all things to be one with the breath

Now that I am at my Mother's breast I know that the breath must go

The ego must drown in the Mother's flow

The River knows, the River knows

The dance begins
In Kashi there is no sin
The seeds of karma cannot take hold
Yet if one has to come to Kashi to sin
He is kept from the Mother until he climbs from eternity and begs to know the River that will fill even the sinner

The moon is full as the dead dance upon the breast of Shyama
The dead shed all that is karma
No need for karma as Kali dances upon her spouse's chest
So still is Shiva, so at rest

This all occurs in Kashi, the city I know best
The smashan is the place of piety and hope
I worship in the cremation ground at the banks of my River
I am the simple one who walks with the Giver
I am the sinner and the saint
I am the pure one
I am the whore
I am the living
I am the one who is no more
I am woman, I am man
I am Kali, I am Shiva
All that I am is in the Ganga, my River

I am God, I am nature
I am one who takes and one who gives
All on the banks of the Gangé
I am the children who play
I am the sadhu who stays
I am the cow that strays
I am that
OM TAT SAT
That which is that

If one can sit by the River and realize that the normal eye
has no access here—nor speech, nor mind
The River can then drench the spirit in the juice and
nectar of the Mother
If one can sit by the River and suckle like a babe
One will forget the world and all the folly of mankind
If one can see the bliss that has no conditions on the faces
of the children playing in the River
He will see that in the conditioned there could be
no happiness

By the River's edge one can find the unconditioned
simply by being
By the River's edge one can find the real self by
swimming in her waters
The River awakens that which is ever awake
That which is rich, full, and abundant is the River
I, the poet of the River Song, can only be humble before
her waters
I drink and beg others to drink

The children playing as they herd the water buffalo are
her favorites

She protects them in their youth and schools them for
life's sorrows

She allows them to carry the waters into tomorrow

And when these children become the sadhus
staying by the River

They drink from their own skulls and are forever full

See

I ask those who first venture to the River's edge

See the candles being placed on the leaves

The River is honored, the River is pleased

And what of the dead who float on the River, asks a new
devotee of the Gangé

Do they scare the children at play?

No, I answer

The children of the River know the River

They make room for the corpse to float on his course or
the course of his Mother

The children, being River children, only know
the River—they know no other

And what of the burning flesh upon the fiery pyres—
Does the scent scare the children and make them cling to life?

The scent of death is carried by the wind to all who
    live or come to the sacred city of Kashi
No one here in the shadows of the golden temples fears death
On the contrary, the River child honors death
    and plays in the River the dead float upon
The scent becomes mingled with the scent of jasmine
    and musk, the River's scent at dusk

Why are there so many old ones dying in the city of Kashi?

I look toward my Mother, the River, and I answer
    with the River reflecting in my eyes,
No one dies of hunger in Kashi
The old are taken care of in Kashi
Annapurna is always there in Kashi
The River takes away the old ones' fear in Kashi
Shiva is always near in Kashi

All can feel what they cannot see in Kashi
The night is always lit by the pyre's light in Kashi
Chaos is undone in the silence of the River in Kashi
The sun is still strong in her dying light in Kashi
All lovers of the linga sing songs until death in Kashi,
songs to Shiva who dwells in Kashi
No one in Kashi can deny the full breast of the River Mother
All dreams of liberation come true in Kashi
One's eyes look upon a brighter sun in Kashi, a lighter night
in Kashi
The River that runs through the city reflects her temples
made of gold in Kashi

One sits on the banks of the River between temple
and temple reflecting on the surface of the River
One knows in that moment that there is certainly a Giver
Old ones cry in bliss
Young lovers feel God's kiss
Babies feed from their mothers' breasts
Children play in her waters and ignore all the rest
No one fears the long night of Kali in Kashi
All dance upon the chest of Shiva in Kashi

My River, you are the light of my heart
  that warms my chela's soul

I shall carry your abundance on the wings of a butterfly

And when the snow starts to melt from way up high
  and the River begins to soak all that is dry

I shall teach of the young bride who followed her Shiva
  up the mountain high

She walked behind him barefoot in the snow

She turned and saw the children playing in the River

The River starts from so high

The child bride started to cry for Kashi

Her consort turned and smiled, saying,

We will leave Kashi only for a little while

Yet we will never leave the River

We will go to her source

We will go to where the soul can never get lost

When we are full and abundant and you with child

We will carry the River once more in my hair to Kashi
  where the River runs wild

Up the mountain they walked
He was Shiva Laxaman
She, the child of the River,
The Mother of all who thirst for the waters
She, the poet,
She, Ganga's daughter

The River must be revealed by those who love her waters
The River must be worshipped in the place of the heart
The River is the life force called prana
It is the upward breath
It is the inward breath
The River is the place of the non-breath
The place of life-giving forces, the place of death
The River is the place of prasad
All that comes from the River is a gift of God
The River is that which is the spine of man
The River has always been—since time began

The pilgrim then gives thanks to his Mother as he goes on
and lives his life
Nothing changes—all is the same
Except the pilgrim dies in life

The worshippers of the Great River dared the night
Dared the night to consume them now that the waters
were in their veins
Nothing is different
Yet once the water is touched, nothing is the same
The fullness of Kashi is the fullness of the Mother's name

Gangé, Gangé, may I come and sit to watch the children play?
The Mother emerges from her own waters
Sits upon her own banks as she blows upon the conch

On hearing the ancient sound they come from all around
They gather at her feet
The waters flow from her toes
Another stream is born
The temple bells ring
The pujari chants her name
The children grow into men and women

The River devours age
The River Song is written on the wind by the sage
Were our bones ever innocent of life?
Were we ever free of karma before the River?
How many deaths, Mother, must one go through to
acknowledge the Giver?

Children keep lying in my waters
The bones will dissolve in time to teach those who come
after you
Our sons and daughters
Sadhu, keep staying by the waters
You will grow old and young as you pray by my wet
All who come to the River are accepted
All who come to the River are blessed

Illusion was formed on the banks of the Ganga
Maya danced with life on the banks of the Ganga
Who will chance life on the banks of the Ganga?
Not all answered *I will*, on the banks of the Ganga

The sadhu chanted, *What is the cause of life and death?*
The sannyasi created the answer from the mind
The jnani accepted the answer and the Word was born
All on the banks of the Ganga forgot the Ganga's song

Children who play in their Mother's waters cannot be wrong
The holy ones stayed on the banks too long

Come, said the River child, *come and play in the Ganga*

Nay, answered the sadhu, *I must stay by the Ganga*

Swim, said the River child to those who roamed in the city
old by the Ganga

No, said the city ones, *we must seek out the temple gold in Kashi*

Give us the ash of the dead, said the River child

Nay, said the brahmin, *the ash is not for play*

The song was forgotten
The tune lost
The Mother flooded the land
None could enter the waters, none could understand

Shiva came from his mountain, tears dripping down his face
Shiva's tears can only bring grace
All must listen to the River child
All must know the heart's wild child
The ash of the dead indeed must be played upon
The world would be too grim if the ash were not
    taken within

Sadhu, come with your Shiva knot high upon your head
Come into the Mother and dance with the dead
Cities who have witnessed all in your years reflecting upon
    the waters of the Mother
Welcome all into your temples of gold
The Mother's story must be told
Cows who stray all the day come into the waters
Let the flesh of those laid to rest
    on the pyres of the Manikarnika Ghat
    wake up dead on the feet of Mother Kali

The River welcomes her children's dreams
The River is much more than she seems
The whole world resides in this land of Kashi
Eternal sleep in this land of Kashi
Waters deep in this world of Kashi
The waters of the Ganga carry the load of the Goddess's feet in this land of Kashi
One cannot be kept in ignorance in this land of Kashi
Take my Mother to heart, says the River child

Shiva came down from the mountain whispering into the wind,
Come into my consort's water
Come drench yourself and swim

He looked at his beloved as he took her hand,
You are the Mother's poet
Write so many can understand
Write on her banks, in her sacred sand
Gather her children and sing your song
Saying this he began to dance

Agni came, flames shooting out
He jumped all around this God-man
All asked in wonder,
How will Shiva dance in the heat of Agni's flames?

Shiva's consort smiled and said, *He will dance saying my name*

All turned toward the Ashen God
He was dancing upon one foot, his lips moving a message to his heart
One word could be heard—
Ma, Ma, Ma

A child sang out, *He is of great body and limb*
Another said, *He calls the Mother from within*
She who is called Bhagavati looked upon her lover and simply smiled
Instead of looking her age, youth came closer to her face than the grave
The fire, the dance, the waters made her look beautiful and fierce
She was laughing as the tears were falling

You who have obtained this priceless birth do not waste it
Live always at her feet
Call every water Gangé
Call every soil Kashi
Call every poem the poem of Kashi Gangé
Watch Shiva's dance on one foot
See in all eyes the look, the look of this priceless life
Spiritual strength shall come to where it is moist
The dry ones live in a hell of their own
Let the dust of the Mother's feet fall into her own waters
    and create the mud of God
In all waters there is the heart
The poem and the poet shall never part
Children who play in my River become the sadhus who stay
    by my River
Shiva, Shiva, only you know how I love my River
Shiva, you are the Giver
I am the receiver
I am the believer
I am Ma

If there were one paradise upon this earth
It would be the place of the Ganga in her city, Kashi
The place where the seeds of karma cannot grow
The place where all the River children know
Of the holy ones who stay by the River
The city old by the River
The temples gold by the River
How the cows stray by the River
All the day by the River

If there were one paradise upon this earth
It would be where Nataraj can dance with one foot raised until the end of his days
Where Kali in the cremation ground can play
Where Tara can row the boat made of bone to the other shore of life
Where the River's waters can flow day and night
Where the tender mango can be eaten
Where the shores of death mingle into the shores of life
Where one can drink from his own skull
Where all can taste God and become whole

I shall teach of this place till my life becomes old
I shall teach of this place till all can find the blanket of
Kashi to keep them warm
I shall teach of this place and the River Song

I am the poet of the River's flow
This I am sure, this I know
I bow to the bull in me
I bow to the sacredness of the neem tree
I beg the naked Naga to always be with me
I dedicate my River Song to the naked Naga who has
always taken form
Always to be at the Mother's feet
Always to die in victory, not defeat
He has lived to protect the Mother
He has died as he has lived, at her feet
The River Song upon his lips sung from his burning heart

It was the Mother who set him free
The Mother—that is me
From the center of the earth
Where Brahma cast down the River Ganga to be caught
by Shiva
Where he sang out the words to all who could hear,
It is no use, I cannot shake her loose
Cannot live with her in my hair
Yet I cannot live if the Mother is not near

In Kashi a man who was bad can become holy and real
In Kashi by the River a man can become free to feel
the flowing waters of Gangé
In Kashi, where a man can learn to play
in the Mother's waters
Drenched in the love for her daughters
One can take one small step at a time
One can become the River's poet without rhythm or rhyme

In this city of Shiva one can learn the truth of the mango
The ambrosia of the gods
Come and take your full drink of her waters
A world without the Ganga is like the earth without the sun

When the rains come, the River rises
The dead are made wet by their Mother Ganga
They do not cry or moan because the River has taken
them home
The dead love Kashi
The dead are Kashi

I sit on the banks of my timeless River
My chelas surround me
My breasts are full
My heart is saturated by the River herself
I drink as I pour
I always drink as I pour

As I give away my River, I am always sure of more
When one is drenched, those around him are drenched too
This is the greatness of the soul
This is the greatness of the River

There is no beginning nor is there an end
The River flows
The children know
The sadhu waits
The cities grow old
The temples shine their gold
The cows stray all the day
Watching the children play

The Guru teaches all who his heart reaches
  You are not this body
  When your mind is absorbed in the River's flow
  You will know, you will know
  You will know the River Song
  It will not take long

Many come to die in our Kashi
Many come to have their ashes float upon her breast
Many come to hear my song
They know it is the River I know best
Yet I must say to all who call themselves
  the Mother's bhaktas
That to know the River is to know me
I shall hold you all as I watch the Naga watching
  the River child play all the day as the cows stray
I shall feed you the River's milk as I sit in the shadow of
  the temples gold as the siddhas grow old in my city
  of Kashi
My ashram, my chelas, have all come to be from a wish
  made by the River, by my Baba, the Naga, and me

We wished upon the wishing neem tree that I, your Ma,
  could set the flowing waters free
Free to just be

I wished as the children were playing in my River
That you would never forget you were the children
    playing in my River
I wished that you would remember it was you who was
    the sadhu staying by my River
I prayed before the sacred dhuni that you would all follow
    your hearts that connected you to the River's flow
I begged my chelas would always know the River's name
    and the River's fame
The Naga learned well and made ready to die
I never asked why

For I knew

Down the mountain they came hand-in-hand
The old woman and the older man
She had the butterfly on her hand
The Naga's form had flown away
    on the wings of that same butterfly

I wished by that River that you would remember
    the heart of the water and always know
    I am your Ma

That I, the poet daughter of the River, shall love you
    till you die

And when death comes upon you
    like the Naga who gave up flesh

You would know there is so much more left

That the River flows through life and death

No more sorrows, no more regrets

I am your Ma

I am, I am

I am everything you are, chela

I am always near, never far

Children, come play by my River
Sadhu, stay by my River
City old by my River
Temple gold by my River
Cows stray all the day by my River
1008 beads on the mala of my River
1008 seeds on the banks of my River
I have given you the song of the Giver
I have given you, chela, my life
I have given you me as I sit drenched in my River
You are my life, chela
You are that for whom I have taken flesh

We, together, shall sing with the naked Naga
the way of the River

Remember how you played by the River?
How the sadhu...